EMOTIVE NAPALM

Ejine Okoroafor

Order this book online at www.trafford.com
or email orders@trafford.com

Most Trafford titles are also available at major online book retailers.

Print information available on the last page.

ISBN: 978-1-4907-7632-3 (sc)
ISBN: 978-1-4907-7631-6 (e)

Trafford rev. 08/17/2016

 www.trafford.com

North America & international
toll-free: 1 888 232 4444 (USA & Canada)
fax: 812 355 4082

FOR MY SISTER

AGBOMA OBIAKU OKOROAFOR

CATHARSIS

The Avenger

Stood, brandishing a righteous sword
Steady jabs of offensive words
Relentless prods for reaction
Resolute pursuit of retribution

Unyielding
Unforgiving
Buoyed by mules
Gingered by folks

Distorted sense of entitlement
Deluded circumstance of birth

Retribution
Castigation
Humiliation
Fabrication

No bounds
No limits

Thin line stripped
As love evolves into hatred

For what?
For naught?

Live by the sword
Die by the sword

The Abuser

His torrential babble
As warped as his mind
As blinded as his fury
As he verbally abuses

Those venomous invectives
Keen on demeaning
Aiming to demoralize
As he emotionally blackmails

His constant play
At stripping your self confidence
At rendering you insecure
And beholden to him

All an epical fail

His initial ploy now botched

Where insults failed, he punches
Where goading failed, he slaps
Where ranting failed, he kicks
He physically abuses

Transformed to a brute
Contorted with rage
Spewing with hate
Battering with rancor

Behold the stranger
Far from the lover
Avowed and committed
To love and protect his bride

His vitriolic exposes him
Every punch betrays his low self esteem
His false sense of bravado reeks of his insecurity
His exploit bares his deceitfulness

Don't let him lay his hands on you
You are not his punching bag
You are not his adversary
You are not combaters

Depart from him
Your dignity intact
Your sanity in place
Your safety ensured

Love and batter
Are never a match
And the strength of a man
Doesn't lie in hitting his woman

His folks should have taught him better

Break-up

Snap, cut loose
Stark, laid bare
Raw, sore
Game, over

Dead end
Unheralded
No harbingers
Sans options

Reprimands
Recriminations
Resurged ire
Regurgitated bile

Concrete
Obtuse
Obstinate
Zero arbitration

Merciless, avenging
Brutal, vengeful
Curt, snappy
Jag, jugular deep

Destruction
Demolition
Extermination
Derogation

On the Flip
Only Hollowness
Pure Sadness
Immense Grief

Packed Pity
Clear view
Of palpable vulnerability
Unmistakable gullibility

Wisp of Eldorado
Could've been
Would've been
Now, never will be!

Who rocked the boat?

Vows on a ledge
Tethered on a rickety pivot
Quivery from the start
Yet resolutely stood

Equilibrium persistently swayed
This way-other way, wavering
Low swing- high swing, equilibration
Brink of collapse occasionally trussed

As spousal merger thrived
On unremitted balance restoration
As experience keeled
For blooming stability

But unbeknownst naysayers came
Familial garb swapped for sheep clothing
From their tumultuous homes
Professing and persuading doom

And nuptial tipped
Nagged and prodded
Into discord and oblivion
Untying knots

Did they rock that boat?
Or did they rock that boat?
For if nurtured and fortified
Might have weathered the storm

Bemused

I am not your mother
You are not your father
We are not your parents
Please don't get us confused

Your mother says do this
Your father says do those?
You say do both
Now y'all got me confused

Naught to offer

Can you understand affection?
That bears no price tag

Would you believe in love?
That derives innately

Can you offer security?
While insecurity ridden

Can you offer happiness?
From a miserable depth

Can you give love?
If you only knew conditional love

Can you
Love for Love?

General Machismo

Yes Sir!
He, who must be obeyed,
Scourging words spewed
Lashing and berating
Denigrating
Stomping
Merciless

Yes Sir!
He, who must not be crossed,
Dare and be damned
Unforgiving elephant
Vengeful
Crushing
Stamping

Yes Sir!
He, who must be adored,
Entitlement is a right
Derived of basal insecurity
Porous
Pompous
Petty

Yes sir!
Thanks sir
Good day sir
The best, the most
The s…! Yes Sir!

DIRGE

Tribute to a Maverick

Of Royal descent Born
Begotten of Princess Idu and iconic Brown
Chip off grandpa Onisa's Block

Fairer than a maiden
Handsomer than Adonis
Sturdier than a pole

Of regal gait and stature
Lithe on the dance floor
Melodious like a Nightingale

An ultimate maverick
Unhampered by modernity
Unconvinced by tradition

Fiery
Feisty
Fearless

You lived by your own system
Called life on your own terms
On balance, destiny's encased on every palm

To strangers, an enigma
To few Intimates, a virtuous force
To us, simply Papa

Loving
Caring
Nurturing

Alas, you were called to the Lord too soon
Albeit, rejoining your Reggie
Abandoning us unwittingly

Agbo-baby!
Eji-girl!
Chu-boy!

We miss you Papa and Big Daddy
We will forever cherish your memory
We wish you peaceful repose in the Lord!

Ode to my mother

You nourished the egg that formed me
Nine months in your womb I lay
Protected and shielded while I matured
Then into the world I was propelled
The link uncut even as the cord was cut
You guided and nurtured me still
Through the maze of my childhood
Guiding me the right way out of the muddle
And even in my teenage days
When I thought I held the world in my palm
You patiently listened and bore with me
You wiped my tears when I cried
You shared my joy when I excelled
You encouraged me when I was low
You stood by me when no one else would
You believed in me even when my dreams
Seemed beyond my scope
You were the rock on which I lay
And when life began to make sense
And an adult I became
With all the virtues you imbibed in me
You left like a tree felled in its prime
The fruit of your labor you never reaped
Guess heaven needed you more than I do
I love you mama and will always do
Your smile is forever encased on my soul
The memories of you is an anchor
That I will rely on for the rest of my life

Cenotaph

Dearest Papa and Mama
To the Lord your departed souls
Reunited, rebounded and to part no more

We've seemingly borne your loses with dignity
Yet our hearts did rage, counter and recriminate
Until we made and found solace in the Almighty
Only he giveth and taketh

Nonetheless, your loss remains no less immense
Nor did our pain become any less intense

We know you're looking out for us
And on our part, we'll strive to do you proud
Your memories are always an anchor
That we'd rely on for the rest of our days

Adieu Dearest Papa and Beloved Mama
May your souls rest in Perfect Peace

Amen!

Indomitable Aunty Val

I am unable to pinpoint our initial meeting
Yet our bond was inevitable and intense
You took me to your bosom
You bore me, no less than a mother would

You were indomitable
Reliable, resilient, infallible
You told it like it was
You told it from the heart

You gave without reservation
You loved without repercussion
Your wisdom was unrivalled
Your enthusiasm was unbridled

You departed without much notice
Swift was the clutch of death
Devastating the aftereffect
As we are left bereft

Unable to comprehend
Difficult to believe
The reality of your demise
The inevitability of death

But our prayers abound
For your peaceful repose
In the bosom of the Lord
Until we meet, to part no more

EMOTIVE NAPALM

Poignant Lamentations

Alas!

When the shocking news broke
A myriad of thoughts and emotions
Ran through our minds

Shock!

Death defines no foe or kin
Shows no peculiar predilection
And is akin to a silent inveterate burglar

Desolation!

Once again, masterful and decisive in strike
Escaping via an assured gateway once deed accomplished
Thereby leaving us bereft and impotent at its latest strike

Frailty!

Despite being pre-armed with the knowledge
That Death is an eventual end to all life and living, inevitable
Yet nothing compares to the reality of losing a loved one

Anger!

Dare we rage against death?
Dare we rage against life that ultimately succumbs to death?
Dare we rage against God?

Bewilderment!

Many thoughts and emotions come to mind
Nonetheless you, Papa believed that destiny is encased in our palms
So maybe, yours has played its hand out

Succor!

We might derive or try to find solace
somehow to uplift our broken spirit
We might try to be or act brave in the face of our broken heartedness
Yet underneath those façades lays our despair

Valuation!

Our devastation at your loss, dearest Papa is immense
A mighty gaping achy hole has been sunk in our lives and mind
As we struggle to grapple with the realism
and finality of your departure

Acceptance!

We however bid you well on your final journey, Papa
We wish that you find everlasting peace and tranquility
As you rejoin our beloved Mama and your Maker

Farewell!

Adieu Papa and Big daddy
May your soul rest in peace
Amen.

LOVE SONGS

Love at first sight

Perfect strangers
Eyes met and locked

You had me from, "hello"

With an irresistible pull
To an invisible magnetic orb
And instant chemistry

Our love blossomed
Unfolding with chats
Unraveling with shared experiences
Enriching with mutual laughter

Like sunrise and spring
Enchanting Petals unfolded
Glorious Birds chimed
As our souls warmed

Our guardedness melted into trust
Skepticism altered into belief
Hesitancy into certainty

And we grow in steadfastness
Perfectly synced imperfections
My Yang complimentary to your ying

Then on bent knees
You bestowed me a ring
I said yes!

Our Future untold, but merged
In a wager for wedlock

For better
For worse
For you and I
The Promise of Eldora
Is the promise for Eternity

Sister, sister

I opened my eyes to the world and to you
A leading beacon from the start of my life
While I lumbered into your hereto haven

You had bewilderedly contended with me
Unsure of what to make of me, this new un-malleable toy
Fast proving to be an unsolicited usurper
Come to stay and to share

I crawled to your walk
And walked to your run
Until we began to speed in tandem

Squabbling and wrangling for toys et al
Haggling for more attention from the folks
A healthy dose of sibling rivalry in tow

Through our ensuing years
We've shared so much
Happy and good times
Some bad and even terrible losses

Leaving our sisterhood no less secure
And our bond no less irrevocable
Our love, no less binding and unconditional

Just so you know,
I wish for none other than you
And if I have to choose over again
I'll choose you over and over again

I love you, Sis

Love

So simple
So real
So love

Inexplicable charm
Undeniable attraction
Ecstatic merger

No premeditation
No calculation
No in-or-convenience

Clear attraction
Deep devotion
Pure bliss

So pure
So surreal
So love?

'Tis the little things

The joyful tinkle of your laughter
The croaked upper lip of your smile
The waft of your favorite perfume
The hesitant shuffle of your dance steps

'Tis the little gestures

The early cuppa of tea in bed
The whole body soft sensuous massage
The cheeky texts that lightens my day
The encouraging words of support

'Tis the love

That strives to commend, not condemn
That tries to accommodate, not exterminate
That wishes to compliment, not compete
That is truly love, not lust

'Tis you

That is me
This is us
The one

Yeah, could be us?

Love Code

Be free
In choice and expression

Be true
In desire and decision

Be real
To self and lover

Stay strong
Stay inspiring
Stay validated
Stay empowered
Stay together
Stay in love

Hesitant

My taut invincible cords of resistance
Persistently anchors for a release
I feel like I'll be falling
Into a ditch strewn with flowers
Your arms outstretched to catch me

Yet I resist a free fall
While still strongly drawn
To your intensifying appeal
To your encouraging words
To your enticing disposition

But my inhibitions fail to depart
For once bitten, twice shy?

Yet will I refuse to rise
For fear of a fall
Will I refuse to take a chance?
For fear of failing

My resistance starts waning
My fears start dwindling

My trust grows
My love buds
My hopes build

How would you handle?
What would you say?
What would you do?
With my heart
If I entrusted it to you

My pledge

I pledge my heart to you
I bare my soul to you
I give my love to you
I take comfort in you
I entrust my happiness to you

I delight in you
I laugh with you
I bond with you
I sing with you
I empathize with you

Today's with you
Tomorrow is for us
I plan a future with you
To age with you
I plan my forever with you

How do you love?

How do you love?
How can you love?
How will you love?

How do you love?
How do you believe love?
How do you understand love?

How do you see love?
How do you show love?
How do you love?

Like a Butterfly

Petite dancer on the floor
Light on her feet
And Lithe

Floating like wind
Caressing the wood with her moves
So Flirty

Stretching out perfect lines
In synch with music and rhymes
And Crisp

Rhythmic hip swings
Sensuous gyrations to music
So Enthralling

Dancing the music
Breezy effortless sway
Nimble like Butterfly

Lose your inhibitions

Just this once
Close your eyes
Lose yourself
Let your imagination take control
Free your inhibitions

Soar
Let yourself loose
Go Limp, surrender
Float freely in the air

Let the wind
Lead and ferry you
To a place unknown
Where you have no cares
No worries
No commitments

Free your spirit
Live for this moment
With Effortless abandon
Savor the moment
Covet this memory

And for Just this moment
Just live!

ANGST

Illusion

I have to contend with this imagery
Relentless mind trick
That keeps playing on my mind
My fervent desire turned to aberration
Pseudocyesis
False pregnancy of desire
Of your formation
A growing bump
Morning sickness
Intermittent baby kick
Another missed period
Lending creed to this illusion
Yet I hold the fervent hope
I maintain a persistent faith
For life will never be whole
Without the reality of you
For now, I hold on
I hold out for that day
When your entrance shall
Enrich and solidify my being

The one who got away

I wander with a heart
Missing a chip
Because you got it
That chip, off my heart
I left it with you
I left it for you
For my heart will never be whole
Loving you
Losing you
Yet you have that chip
A little bit of my heart
You hold it
You take it
For you will always be a part
Of me
The scar on my heart
Will always remind me of you
So keep that chip
And I hope it reminds you of me

Supplication

I never needed anything more
I never prayed harder for anything
I refuse to give up the hope for you

I hold steadfast hope for you
I fervently believe the miracle of you
I await the reality of you

When the double lines will show
When the stomach bump will protrude
When your joyful wail will screech

Oh what bond?
Oh what joy?
Oh how amazing?

Just how beautiful, life will be
Oh how complete, my life will be
O how amazing, the miracle of God

I continue to hope and pray
For that day, someday soon
When you'll be laid in my hands to love and cherish

Unrequited love

Oh what pain?
The anguish of a tortured heart
The expense of love unrequited
Unreciprocated affection
Unanswered fervor

Oh what hope?
The unfulfilled desire for reciprocation
The hunger for amity
Love in isolation
Lost in translation

Oh what agony?
The relentless drive for commitment
The burden of love unrequited
Unmet needs
Mismatched mates

Doomed

You smile
A tortured grin
From a tormented soul
You stay stoic
True to your promise
True to your vows

I watch helplessly
My heart bleeds
My soul aches at your torment
At your haplessness
At my helplessness
And inability to untangle you

You continue to dance
The wretched rave
Of one-sided love
The misstep of
An undeserving lover
The music of the fated

Memoir

In the book of my life
You'd make a chapter
Because you were a part
Of whom I am
Of the person I became

You stomped the pathway of my heart
Leaving an indelible scar
A constant reminder
Of what could have been
Of dreams unfulfilled

While we might have failed to walk together
While we failed to stay together
While we failed to fulfill those dreams
While we broke those vows
While we severed ties

I still remember our days together
I still retain the memories we made
I still recall the moments that we shared

I'll forever cherish them
The soil of my soul knows
You did trod its path

Ex Factor

I peered at your familiar figure
Clearly there was you and her
You barely took note of me
You were too engrossed

I couldn't help but watch
And notice how you held her
How you stooped to help
Get the pebble off her feet

Your laughter was loud
Pealing clearly
Like you had no care
To the world and I

It was different
It looked special
It was obvious
That you cared deeply

Never known you so tender
Never seen you smile so widely
Never knew you so merry
Never heard you laugh so heartily

It made my night
To observe your happiness
To hear the joy in your laughter
To behold your soulmate

I wish you the best
For when love is right, it's right
When love meets love, it's magic
And may you both stay magical

FOLKLORE

Elegy of a fostered kid

Hello Mummy?

I keep imagining
Nestling in your womb
Your gradually growing bulge
My rippling kicks
A reminder of my being
As I strengthened into life

Was I lovingly made?
Or accidentally conceived?
Did you stroke your bump?
Wonder about the miracle of me?
Did you envisage me?
Imagining if I'd look like you?

I keep imagining

You bearing me
My wailing entrance
Heralding my arrival
Your trailing placenta
A reminder of our link and connection

What was your initial thought?
At the first sight of me?

Did you cuddle me to your chest?
Did our hearts beat fast in tandem?
Did you suckle me to your breast?
Did your emotions overflow with joy?

I keep imagining
At what point, you made up your mind
To give me away
What turned you off me?
Was it the conception of me?
Was my shrieking entrance too off putting?
Was it ....?

I keep imagining
Million imageries
Billion queries

I imagine you
I imagine me
As a replica of you

Please wipe that smirk.....

I am a mother of four
From four different fathers

Till you hear my full story
Till you walk in my shoes

Then you can judge
Then you can bear your smirk

My great grandmother
She was born a slave

She served her master
Both at labor and in bed

My grandmother was born
Never acknowledged by her father

She lived in another farm
And served her master in labor and bed

My mother, she was feisty
Ran away from the farm

She went to the city
There she met Joe

Joe was a pimp
Preached her a better life

She took up Joe for his word
But he only pimped her out

So I was conceived
Father unknown

For the many men she lay
Neither she, nor Joe knew which my father was

My earliest memories
Were of a drugged mother and violent Joe

Mama was beholden to Joe
He beat her to pulp

He cajoled me to quiet
And put me to work as soon as he could

Had my first baby at fourteen
It was a miracle how he survived

After my second at sixteen
We made a run for the safe haven

Without a good education and no job
I soon resorted back to my old trade

Then third pregnancy and baby
Before my epiphany

Finally got my act together
After I found a good man and God

Got back to school
Set up my business

Thrived in love and family
Had another baby for my man

Yes I am a mother of four
From four different fathers

Sick

I've got the bug
No, not the cold
But of the crave
The persistent hanker
That seems to absorb me
I must quench it
I must drink it
I must smoke it
I must inject it
I must sniff it

Yes, that type of bug
I've let it burrow into me
I let it latch unto me
Such that
I can't shake it out
I can't cut it out
It's stuck on me
It's in my blood
It's running through my veins
It's a disease
And I need a cure

Another glass in hand
The last shot, I promise
That pang, irresistible
Deep unquenchable hole
A draining hole
Porous, glass after glass

Beer, liquor, cognac
I gulp at any beverage
Filling my hole
Drowning my soul
That's my sickness

My name is Joe
And I am an addict

COQUETRIES

Dangerous liaison

Flickering candle
Golden globe beckons
Flies to fire
Burnt
Yet irresistibly drawn

Dangerous liaison
Irresistibly drawn
Smoldering Passion
Spent
Yet Affianced

Cat and mouse
Irresistible attraction
Maddening
Cat-a-mousing
Vicious cycle

Moi et Tu
Poles apart
Drawn
Cataclysmic
Unholy union

Side show

He's got his woman
She's got her man
They got a side show
They are both kicking with others

Stolen moments
Thrill of deceit
Rush of guilt
Effervescent lust

He returns to his woman
She returns to her man
They return to life
Living like normal

Living a lie
Ten years later
He is still with his woman
She's so bad that he can't give her up

She sticks by her man
Who treats her so bad that she can't leave?
Ten years later, they are still together
They are still cutting it, side show!

Bobo nkiti

Bo-bo *nkiti*
Fine boy, no pimple
Uwa ana aso gi!

Omaricha nwa
God's own gift to woman
O na afuo!

Man about town
iwelu na efe obodo
Chicks *ana* flock your side

Oriri na mmanya
Chicks *ana eweta ego*
Kedu kwa nu ife ha cho ka ime?

Nkwari
Sugar mummies abound
Uwa ga na aga kwanu

Bobo ga dinu on
Chicks *ga na ewete ife*
Onwe?
Mbanu,
O Bobo-nkiti

Booty Call

He calls with only a few minutes to spare
But he's got you on his mind
Like ever, and always

He only shows up when he's in your vicinity
Crawling up to your crib
In time enough for a quickie

He reiterates that there's really no one like you
He loves you, he cares
You are his best

He vanishes again into thin air
No calls, no word
Until he stops by again, for a quick one

You are still not clear to his game
He might be good in the sack
But he's made you, his booty call

ABODES

Weep not for Oguta

Once upon a time
In our blue peninsula
We all lived like family
We all loved like brothers

We sang in unison
We danced in unity
We ate from same bowl
We relished our glorious land

The land of the virtuous
The magnificent city of Ameshi

Until evil reared its head
Unfounded Anarchy set in
Uhamiri rumbled
Overflowing its banks

Brothers turned against brothers
Mayhem became the day's order
Accusations and counter accusations
Reverberations and massacring

We played to the devilish chord
We heeded to those that loved to hate us
They ignited our fire
Lending creed to our chaos

The turmoil came to a head
Tragic demise of an honorable legend, in tow

An uneasy calm set
More ominous than the rumble

The tide ebbed
Urashi receded
Ties became porous
Trust was lost
Brother's no more?

Events took their brunt
Blue water bloodied
Land soiled
Whither now?

Is all our glory forever gone?
Is all beauty entirely wilted?
Is our brotherhood irrevocably shattered?
Is all hope totally lost?

Nay, sayeth the Patriots
Arise, they bid
A clarion call for all
To regain our glory

To nudge our broken fold to life
To re-mould our foundation
To reshape our future
To nurture our youth

Arise, o brethren
For we are as strong as our weakest link
Let's buoy our culture
Help empower our youth
And resuscitate our glory

Arise Umu Ameshi
Kudos to the Patriots
Long Live Oguta
Forever obodo giri giri
Ndi oma, ndi oma

Weep not for Oguta

Tale of 4 cities

Rainy
Sunny
Snowy
In equal measures
Coast to coast
Hopes and Dreams equalize
God Bless America

Balmy
Rainy
Blighty
Of airs and graces
Curtsies and crowns
More of Hopes than Dreams
God save the Queen

Sunny
Icy
Wintery
In extremes and exigencies
Republic to Republic
Devoid of Dreams and Hopes
From Russia, with love

Sunlit
Humid
Tropic
Of unenhanced Assets
Tribe to tribe
Of Dashed Hopes and Dreams
Nigeria, we hail thee

Harlem

Hub of Afro-centricity
Anchored by East / Hudson Rivers
Renaissance gateway
Landmark of the black migration era
Emblem of the civil rights movement
Mantle of Afro-culture

Acknowledgement

I've always been more expressive in written than spoken words, thus poetry has always proven to be a needed escape and solace.

This collection of poems were penned at various points in the last decade (circa 2009 – 2016), through traumatic, challenging and exhilarating experiences in my life and in the world generally.

First and Foremost, I acknowledge our indefatigable Almighty Father for his continued mercy.

I dedicate this tome to my beloved sister, Agboma Obiaku Yvonne Okoroafor in commemoration of our beloved late parents and our eternal bond.

I'll also use this opportunity to acknowledge Lauretta Akwule, Ngozi Udom-Ndokwu, Willy Philias, Eze Ugwueze, Ngozi Bell, Elsie Dania, Amede Chukwuma, Chikezie & Nnenaya Duke, Emma & Chinwe Nwapa, and Ifeanyi & Nkemdilim Okoroafor.

Just as these poems encapsulate my emotions and solace, I hope that you are able to derive inspiration and solace from them.

Thank you!

About the Author

Ejine Okoroafor, also previously known as Ejine Okoroafor-Ezediaro, was born and raised in Nigeria. She had obtained a BSc from the University of Port-Harcourt, Nigeria, before studying medicine in Ukraine. She had subsequently practiced internal medicine in various hospitals in the NHS in the United Kingdom for a few years prior to relocating to the USA.

She has since completed a psychiatry residency program at the University of Columbia at Harlem Hospital Center, New York, and psychosomatic fellowship program at the New York Medical College-Westchester Medical Center, Valhalla , New York. She is currently living and practicing psychiatry in Las Vegas.

Ejine's flair for prose and poetry was evident from childhood. She attributes her love for the literary arts to her beloved late mother, Madam Regina Akpara Okoroafor, who was a dynamic literature and French tutor. Her mother had kindled a great interest and love in reading books in her right from a very early age.

Her academic and professional pursuits notwithstanding, Ejine endorses a curious void, which only her passion for writing has begun to fill. This passion has also culminated in the publication of her four books. This includes A Rose in Bloom and Pathos of a Wilting Rose (prequel and sequel novel series respectively); Whimsical Rhapsody (poetry collection); and Inem's folklore series, The Tortoise and the Birds (children's book). A recurring theme in her books includes cultural preservation, emancipation, and equity of our society.

Ejine is also an avid traveler. She has lived in four different countries and travelled to over thirty others. She notes that we as people of the world are very similar in our needs and aspirations, albeit with individual peculiarities, yet tend to expand our differences than embrace our similarities.